Watch It Grow
CORAL REEF

Written by
Kate Scarborough

Illustrated by
Michael J. Woods

How Coral Forms

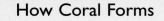

The tiny egg of
a coral animal
drifts in the sea.

A young coral
animal grows
from the egg.

The coral animal
settles on rock
and grows
a skeleton
outside its
soft body.

**The remains
of a turtle**

Eleven Hundred Years Ago

Coral looks like rock, but it is made from the skeletons of tiny animals. These animals live in warm, shallow waters close to the shore.

This reef begins to grow off an island in the Caribbean.

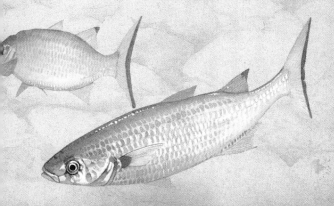

White mullet like to feed in shallow waters.

Inside a Coral Animal

This is the body of one coral animal. It is called a polyp. It has a mouth and tentacles and protects itself by growing a hard skeleton around its soft body.

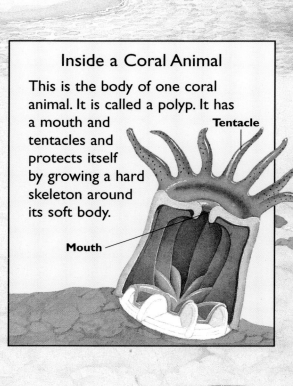

Tentacle

Mouth

A THOUSAND YEARS AGO

The tiny coral animals attach themselves firmly onto the sea floor where they begin to feed and grow.

Single coral animals are tiny. Thousands of them make up a single colony.

White tip shark

New Coral

Some coral polyps split into two to make new polyps.

The new polyps grow next to each other and they both grow a new skeleton.

Other coral polyps make eggs which are released into the water.

NINE HUNDRED YEARS AGO

Coral polyps build into a solid shape. New coral polyps grow on top of the hard skeletons of the old coral polyps that have died.

Flying fish

Sand tiger shark

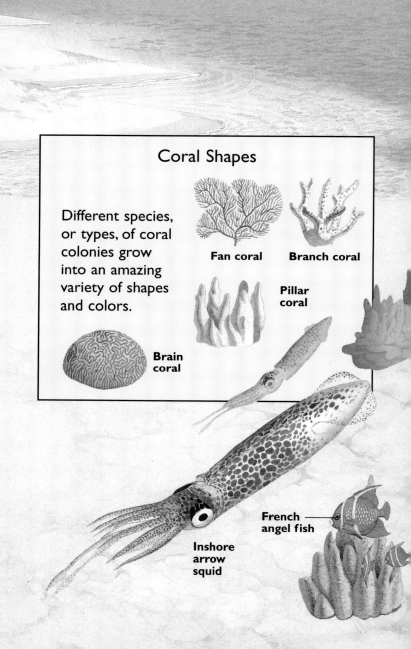

Coral Shapes

Different species, or types, of coral colonies grow into an amazing variety of shapes and colors.

Fan coral

Branch coral

Pillar coral

Brain coral

French angel fish

Inshore arrow squid

Eight Hundred Years Ago

Coral grows in different groups. Each one is called a colony. All the separate colonies together start to make up a coral reef.

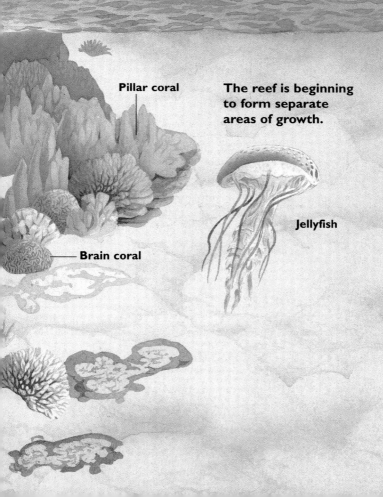

Pillar coral

The reef is beginning to form separate areas of growth.

Jellyfish

Brain coral

Coral Borers

Inside a coral reef, there are tiny creatures that force their way through by making holes. These holes are very important because they fill up with mud and sand, making the coral even stronger.

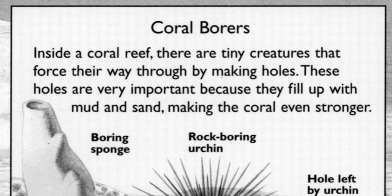

Boring sponge

Rock-boring urchin

Hole left by urchin

The lagoon

Reef shark

SEVEN HUNDRED YEARS AGO

As time goes by the reef gets larger and heavier. All the skeletons of the first coral polyps get crushed slowly by the weight and form a solid layer. This layer can become as solid as rock.

The reef crest

The reef slope

Graysby

Comb grouper

As the centuries pass more and more varieties of coral, plants, and fish settle around the island.

Atoll Reef

Reef circles volcano

Volcano sinks

Atoll remains

Hogfish

Finger coral

Another type of coral reef forms all the way around an island. As the years pass, a volcanic island can sink back into the sea, leaving behind the coral reef that formed around it. This kind of reef is called an atoll reef. The coral has grown steep sides so that the living crest is still in the shallow water.

SIX HUNDRED YEARS AGO

The coral has now formed a fringe that follows the curve of the shore. This reef is called a fringing reef. There is a great variety of fish and other animals here.

Parts of the reef start to break the surface of the water.

Elkhorn coral

The reef now supplies a variety of animals with food.

Cero

Redband parrotfish

Cactus coral

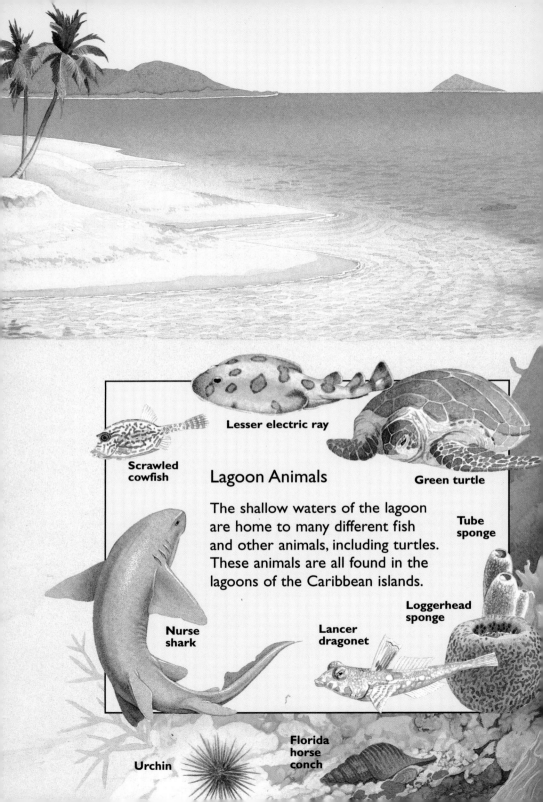

Lesser electric ray

Scrawled cowfish

Green turtle

Tube sponge

Lagoon Animals

The shallow waters of the lagoon are home to many different fish and other animals, including turtles. These animals are all found in the lagoons of the Caribbean islands.

Loggerhead sponge

Nurse shark

Lancer dragonet

Urchin

Florida horse conch

FIVE HUNDRED YEARS AGO

As the reef becomes larger, more animals live around it. Different animals live in each part of the reef. Some live in the shallow waters near the shore, while others stay in the deeper waters.

The reef crest

The wave motion over the crest becomes more vigorous as more of the crest breaks the surface.

Blade fire coral

Star coral

Brain coral

Fourspot butterflyfish

Mottled red sea star

Algae

Because the crest is regularly hit by waves, not many types of coral grow here. However, seaweedlike plants called algae grow.

Box fire coral

Algae

Orange ball sponge

FOUR HUNDRED YEARS AGO

The part of the reef nearest the water's surface is called the reef crest. As the water rises and falls with the tide the crest spends some time out of water.

A ship called a Spanish galleon sails away from the coral reef.

Lettuce coral

Marbled jellyfish

Smooth star coral

Golden hamlet

Green moray eel

Bleached Coral

Some parts of the coral reef have lost all their color. This is called bleaching. Most bleached coral dies. No one is sure why bleaching happens.

Common octopus

Rose coral

Airplane

Sail boat

Fifty Years Ago

The part of the reef that drops down to the seabed is the reef slope. The upper part is crammed with corals and algae. Here a large number of fish feed from among the coral.

Staghorn coral

Brain coral

Orange spot triggerfish

Finger Coral

Encrusting star coral

Clown fish

Reef butterfly fish

Sponge

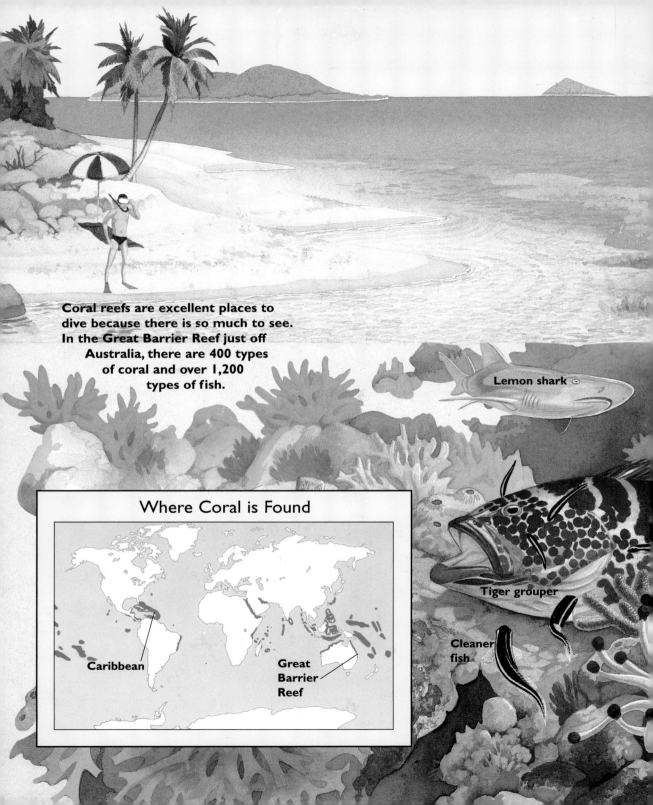

Coral reefs are excellent places to dive because there is so much to see. In the Great Barrier Reef just off Australia, there are 400 types of coral and over 1,200 types of fish.

Lemon shark

Tiger grouper

Cleaner fish

Where Coral is Found

Caribbean

Great Barrier Reef